PHOTOS THAT MADE
U.S. HISTORY

PHOTOS THAT MADE
U.S. HISTORY

Volume 2: From the Cold War to the Space Age

· *Edward Wakin* ·

with Daniel Wakin

WALKER AND COMPANY
NEW YORK

First published in the United States of America in 1993 by Walker Publishing Company, Inc.

Published simultaneously in Canada by Thomas Allen & Son Canada, Limited, Markham, Ontario

Library of Congress Cataloging-in-Publication Data
Wakin, Edward.
Photos that made U.S. history/Edward Wakin with Daniel Wakin.
p.   cm.
Includes index.
Contents: v. 1. From the Civil War era to the atomic age—v. 2. From
the Cold War to the space age.
Summary: Presents photographs (and their stories) that became
almost as famous as the history-making events they depicted.
Includes Lincoln, Nixon and Krushchev, Iwo Jima, Kent State, and
others.
ISBN 0-8027-8230-2 (v. 1).—ISBN 0-8027-8231-0 (lib. bdg. : v.
1).—ISBN 0-8027-8270-1 (v. 2).—ISBN 0-8027-8272-8 (lib. bdg. :
v. 2)
1. United States—History—1865–   —Pictorial works—Juvenile
literature.   2. Photography—United States—History—Juvenile
literature.   [1. United States—History—1865– 2. Photography—
History.]   I. Wakin, Daniel.   II. Title.
E661.W32   1993
973.9′022′2—dc20   93-12096
CIP
AC

Designed by Brandon Kruse
Printed in Mexico

2   4   6   8   10   9   7   5   3   1

Contents

Photographs

Introduction

AERIAL SURVEILLANCE PHOTOGRAPHS that pushed the world to the nuclear brink . . .

A shameful shot of a police dog attacking a helpless teenager at a civil rights march . . .

A "kitchen debate" between U.S. vice president Richard Nixon and Soviet premier Nikita Khrushchev . . .

A shocking photo of an execution on a Saigon street . . .

An unprecedented view from outer space of our solitary planet . . .

When it comes to making as well as recording history, the camera has demonstrated that it can be mightier than the pen. At crucial moments in U.S. history, the photograph has been both a punctuation point and an animating force.

As punctuation point, a photograph has marked off a major episode, a historic part of our past.

As an animating force, a photograph can influence, shape, and direct public reaction and in this way help to make history.

This book will show history-making photographs and tell the story of how they helped to make history. Each photograph is worth seeing on its own merits and also depicts events important to know in order to understand ourselves as a people and as a nation.

Photography's history-recording and history-making dates from its invention in the 1830s. The photographer has acted as witness, the photograph as evidence. The public has responded as judge and jury, pronouncing sentence by the way it reacted.

By influencing the way Americans vote, act, and join (or don't join) in national efforts, these photos have helped to make U.S. history. Looking at the images in this book means coming face to face with our history while it was being made. The experience expands our understanding of who we are and how we as a nation have reached this point.

Each history-making photograph has four elements, which are intertwined, but also separate.

1. *The Event:* What was happening directly involved Americans, and they were caught up in the situation and the circumstances. What was happening both involved and affected them. They were part of the action.

2. *The Image:* The photographs captured what was happening as only a picture can. They cut through thousands of words, eliminated complications, overrode arguments for and against, pushed aside second thoughts. They made Americans at the time and Americans today feel what they saw. The images cut to the quick, said it all—almost.

3. *The Effect:* Something happened because of these photo-

graphs. Americans changed the way they felt; government leaders were stopped in their tracks; votes, laws, decisions were influenced, even shaped. All of this happened within a historical setting. The context and the circumstances turned the image into a history-maker.

4. *The Photographer:* The hand that held the camera did much more than push the button. The attentive eye, the responsive heart, and the alert mind came into play. These photographs celebrate photography and the men and women who dedicate themselves to enabling us to see the world and to help us grasp it.

In looking—really looking—at these photographs, we gain a double return. First, we come into contact with powerful images, appreciated for their own sake and experienced as part of the visual world that surrounds us. Second, we see U.S. history as something alive.

What is history but a story of what men and women do for themselves and to themselves—through war and peace, campaigns and elections, fads, fashions, and social movements? It's a story of how people live during and through different times in different ways.

But what a story!

Since the middle of the last century, it's been a story accompanied by pictures. Here are some that did more than help tell the story: They helped to make it.

PHOTOS THAT MADE
U.S. HISTORY

The Kitchen Debate (July 24, 1959) by Elliott Erwitt.
(Magnum Photos, Inc.)

· 1 ·

"The Man Who Stood Up to Khrushchev"

Strengthening Richard Nixon's
Anti-Communist Reputation

AT THE WHITE railing in front of the model American kitchen at a U.S. industrial exhibition in Moscow, Soviet Communist party chairman Nikita Khrushchev was arguing eyeball-to-eyeball with U.S. vice president Richard M. Nixon.

As *Life* magazine described that incredible day in July 1959: "In the tense exchanges between East and West throughout the cold war there had never been anything like" the argument they were having.

Life added that "the running argument was overheard by the whole world." It was also seen by the whole world in front-page photographs.

A mushroom cloud hung over the argument. Khrushchev and Nixon represented the world's two superpowers, who were enemies in a cold war. Each nation could destroy the other—as well as the rest of the world—with its nuclear weapons. This threat of mutual destruction kept nations on edge as diplomats debated and the world worried.

Nixon had flown to Moscow to open the first United States exhibition ever held in the Soviet Union. Khrushchev was his host. Each was determined to upstage the other.

Nixon later recalled that he "was keyed up and ready for battle as the flight neared Moscow." He had been warned in advance that Khrushchev was a blunt man always ready to argue. He talked tough and liked to bully his opponent.

Before leaving for Moscow, Nixon visited John Foster Dulles, who as U.S. secretary of state led the Western effort to hold back communism. In his memoirs, Nixon recalls Dulles's advice: "You don't have to convince him [Khrushchev] that we are for peace. He knows that. You have to convince him that he cannot win a war."

At their first meeting, at the Kremlin on the morning of July 24, Khrushchev lived up to his reputation. Red-faced and shouting, he denounced the U.S. proclamation of Captive Nations Week, which urged Americans to pray for the people under Communist tyranny. Khrushchev said the proclamation "stinks."

Next, Khrushchev and Nixon drove to the U.S. exhibition, which was opening that evening. At the RCA color TV exhibit, Khrushchev continued to argue as cameras rolled. He boasted: "When we catch up to you, in passing you we will wave to you." He did most of the talking and constantly interrupted Nixon.

They moved on to a model house, where their war of words was waged in front of a model kitchen. Hence the label "Kitchen Debate."

Scores of stunned officials, security guards, and reporters

crowded around the two men. Nixon and Khrushchev argued over who could afford the model house and about the many kinds of washing machines available to Americans. (Khrushchev argued that it was inefficient to make so many different kinds of washing machines.)

The New York Times reported that "the day seemed more like an event dreamed up by a Hollywood script writer than a confrontation of two of the world's leading statesmen."

It wasn't kitchens and washing machines they were actually arguing about, but two ways of life that confronted each other: the Soviet way of state control and communism versus the American way of free-enterprise capitalism and democracy. They were also playing out the competition between the two superpowers, which were in an uneasy nuclear standoff.

At one point, Nixon warned about the danger of an "ultimatum" involving the Soviet Union and the United States: "You are playing with the most destructive force in the world."

Khrushchev flared up and wagged a finger in Nixon's face: "We too are giants. If you want to threaten, we will answer threat with threat."

By this time, both men were jabbing fingers at each other, and photography entered the fray with the assistance of a press agent named William Safire (who later became President Nixon's speechwriter and after that a columnist for *The New York Times*).

Safire took the Associated Press photo that went 'round a jittery world. He also paved the way for photographer Elliott Erwitt to take the memorable *Life* and *Time* magazine photographs that defined the electric moment of the "Kitchen Debate."

In the crush of people surrounding Nixon and Khrushchev,

the AP photographer couldn't get into position to take a photograph. He was stuck in the crowd.

In desperation, the AP photographer tossed his bulky Speed Graphic camera over the heads of Nixon and Khrushchev to Safire, who could get clear of the crowd. Safire quickly took a photograph and lobbed the camera back.

Suddenly, he heard the photographer shouting, "You had your hand over the aperture, you idiot!"

Back came the camera. Safire took a photograph again, making sure to include the washing machine in order to get publicity for the exhibit and his client.

This was the AP wire photo that appeared on the front page of almost every newspaper in the world. It showed Khrushchev listening—for a change—as Nixon spoke and used his hands for emphasis. As Safire later recalled in his book about Nixon, the AP photo showed Khrushchev "getting the worse of the debate."

In addition, Safire had helped photographer Erwitt get inside the exhibit. Erwitt, who was there to get photos of Russians looking at U.S. consumer goods, seized the opportunity. He took what photography historian Vicki Goldberg properly calls a picture that "has all the power of the perfectly captured moment."

It shows Nixon jabbing his finger at Khrushchev—a close-up of the East-West confrontation. Nixon looks determined. Khrushchev looks silenced by what he's hearing. The man in between—undoubtedly a translator—shows by his intense look that the words are serious and emotional. The message received around the world, particularly in the United States, was that Nixon was "The Man Who Stood Up to Khrushchev."

The trip and the photographs scored political points for Nixon. He had his eye on winning the 1960 Republican nomination for president, and then the election. To win the nomination, he had to beat out Nelson Rockefeller, governor of New York.

A few months before the Moscow trip, Nixon was ahead of Rockefeller in the polls, 52 percent to 28 percent. A few months after the trip, his advantage soared. He was ahead by 72 percent to 21 percent. As the McClure Newspaper Syndicate commented after sampling public opinion, "Nixon's presidential prospects have been increased tremendously by his Russian visit."

Once Nixon won the Republican nomination in 1960, Erwitt's picture took on additional life as a campaign photo. It strengthened the image of Nixon as someone who was tough on the Communist enemy. Nixon's Democratic opponent for president, John F. Kennedy, had to match the image with a tough stand against communism. While Nixon narrowly lost the 1960 election to Kennedy, the power of Erwitt's photo as a political weapon was confirmed.

Erwitt has recalled what happened when his photograph became a Nixon campaign poster: "They must have made a million copies of it. There were even murals—all made from that damn 8 × 10. I think it was the most widely known campaign photograph ever."

Pictorial Proof (October 25, 1962). *(AP/Wide World Photos)*

· 2 ·

"We Have Proof and Will Show It to You"

· ■ · ■ · ■ ·

*Confronting the Cuban
Missile Crisis*

THE PRESIDENT OF the United States was soaking in his bathtub while his national security adviser briefed him about the most dangerous photographs ever taken.

They were "hard photographic evidence" based on 30,000 feet of film shot by high-flying U.S. surveillance planes. The photographs proved that the Soviet Union was building missile bases on Cuba that could launch nuclear attacks upon the United States.

On that Tuesday, October 16, 1962, when national security adviser McGeorge Bundy described the photographic evidence to President John F. Kennedy, the world began moving toward a nuclear confrontation.

All members of President Kennedy's administration "were aware that the Soviet leaders had the power to blow America off the face of the earth," recalls George W. Ball, who was then U.S. under secretary of state.

And the United States had the power to do the same to the Soviet Union.

As recollected by the president's brother, Attorney General Robert F. Kennedy, the photographic discovery of the bases marked "the beginning of the Cuban missile crisis—a confrontation between the two giant atomic nations . . . which brought the world to the abyss of nuclear destruction and the end of mankind."

The Soviet Union had smuggled into Cuba medium-range missiles that could launch a nuclear attack upon the United States. Twenty-two thousand Soviet troops and technicians had been sent to assemble the missiles and operate the bases.

The Soviet Union had tricked the United States into thinking that the missile sites were no threat, that they were there only to protect the island of Cuba. The aerial photography exposed the trick and the lie. The missile sites were capable of attacking the United States.

That morning in his bathtub, the president faced a menace and a monumental risk. To eliminate the menace of missiles ninety miles off the U.S. coastline, the president faced the risk of starting a nuclear war.

This was a young president whose toughness Soviet premier Nikita Khrushchev was testing by smuggling missiles into Cuba. This was also a president who understood the stakes. Once, when a newspaper publisher urged him to get tougher with the Russians, he answered by saying:

"I'm just as tough as you are, but the difference between you and me is that I was elected president of this country and you were not. And I have the responsibility of the lives of a hundred and eighty million Americans, which you have not."

That sense of responsibility was tested by the thirteen days of the Cuban missile crisis. They were days of anguish, assessment, and argument; days of uncertainty, confrontation, and negotiation.

Kennedy assembled a group of fifteen advisers and ordered them to "make a prompt and intensive survey of the dangers of all possible courses of action." The advisers met daily, often several times a day, in maximum secrecy. The crisis was being kept from the American public until a decision was made on what to do.

The president's military advisers urged him to launch an air attack on Cuba, followed by an invasion if necessary. Other, more cautious advisers argued for a naval blockade of Cuba, what came to be called a quarantine.

During the painful process of making a decision, the president followed a normal schedule. He even helped campaign for Democratic candidates in advance of November congressional elections. He didn't want to alarm the country or tip his hand to the Russians.

As his advisers talked, the president listened and agonized over what to do. A decision had to be made, and it was his alone to make. At one point, he went to the family's seaside retreat in Hyannisport, Massachusetts, where he walked the beach and pondered his decision. He heard more advice from the generals and admirals who flew there to urge him to attack Cuba.

Next, the president went to Chicago on a campaign trip, still keeping up appearances that everything was normal. His brother Robert phoned from Washington. His advisers were still divided.

Time was running out for a decision. He should come back to Washington.

The president returned and listened to his brother's account of what the advisers wanted him to do. Then he stated his decision simply and firmly: "It's going to be a blockade."

On Monday, October 22, at seven P.M., President Kennedy went on television to tell the American public for the first time what the Soviet Union had done and what he was going to do.

On that day, all American missile crews were placed on maximum alert and all military commands were placed on the highest state of readiness next to war. Ninety B-52s were flying over the Atlantic carrying multimegaton bombs. Nuclear warheads were activated on one hundred Atlas, fifty Titan, and twelve Minuteman missiles and on U.S. carriers, submarines, and overseas bases.

In his television address, Kennedy called the Soviet Union's action in Cuba "deliberately provocative." He warned that it "cannot be accepted by this country," and he announced a naval blockade of Cuba.

At ten A.M., Wednesday morning, October 24, President Kennedy signed the proclamation that imposed the blockade.

Nineteen U.S. ships formed an arc in the international waters five hundred miles from Cuba.

Twenty-five Soviet ships were approaching them.

The U.S. ships had orders to stop the first Soviet ship that had a cargo hold deep enough to carry a missile.

At the signing of the proclamation, two Soviet ships, the *Gagarin* and the *Komiles*, were within a few miles of the circle of U.S.

ships. Between them, a Soviet submarine was moving into position.

At the White House, the president's advisers were meeting. And waiting.

Robert Kennedy described his brother and the question haunting him: "Was the world on the brink of a holocaust?" Would Soviet ships force a confrontation? Would U.S. attacks on the Soviet ships start a chain reaction leading to nuclear war?

President Kennedy waited. "His hand went up to his face and covered his mouth. He opened and closed his fist. His face seemed drawn, his eyes pained. . . . He . . . no longer had control of events."

Then the message arrived that brought matters to a standstill: The Russian ships had "stopped dead in the water."

But the crisis was not over. There were still Soviet bases and missiles in Cuba. Although they were not ready to operate, they remained a threat at America's doorstep, and the United States was determined to get rid of the threat.

Thus began tense negotiations between the United States and the Soviet Union. There were secret messages and contacts, and there was a dramatic public confrontation at the United Nations.

On the evening of October 25, during an emergency session of the United Nations Security Council, the U.S. delegate, Adlai Stevenson, confronted the Soviet delegate, Valerian A. Zorin. He challenged the Russian to deny that the Soviet Union was building the missile sites in Cuba.

"We have proof and will show it to you," Stevenson announced.

Easels were brought into the Security Council to display the aerial photographs to the world. The photographs made history as the proof that triggered the Cuban missile crisis.

The accompanying Associated Press photograph portrays the dramatic scene at the United Nations. Grim-faced, dark-suited diplomats surround the easel, which dominates the photograph. Some diplomats are seated in their roles as U.N. officials or representatives of their countries. Others are standing alongside the easel, some behind it. The camera stops the diplomats in their tracks as they confront an awesome threat with the rhetoric and tactics of diplomacy.

The details add to the tension. Two diplomats confer intently. Another holds his head with his right hand. Behind the easel, a solitary man presses his hand against his mouth. The men watch and listen as U.S. delegate Stevenson shows the proof.

The photograph also contains an accidental comment: A mural on the wall shows human figures looking away from the scene of diplomats confronting the nuclear threat. It is as if humanity can't bear to look.

At the United Nations, Stevenson was blunt. He introduced a U.N. resolution calling for the "immediate dismantling and withdrawal" from Cuba of all missiles and other offensive weapons. He called the day a "solemn and significant" one for "the hope of the world community." He pleaded that it not be remembered "as the day when the world came to the edge of nuclear war."

Fortunately, behind the charges and the denials, an undercurrent of good sense, realism, and responsibility was at work as messages passed between Kennedy and Khrushchev. Neither wanted to let matters get out of hand and provoke a nuclear war.

Two days after the Stevenson speech, Khrushchev wrote Kennedy that he understood "perfectly well" that "if we attack you, you respond the same way."

The thirteen days that shook the world ended when the Soviet Union agreed to remove the Cuban missile bases, and the United States agreed not to invade Cuba.

The Soviet agreement was announced in a special radio bulletin from Moscow on Sunday morning at nine o'clock.

One hour later, a relieved President Kennedy was attending a church service. He turned to his aide, Dave Powers, and said, "Dave, this morning we have extra reason to pray."

To the Attack (May 3, 1963). (AP/Wide World Photos)

· 3 ·

"We Shall Overcome"

Winning Support for Civil Rights

"SING, CHILDREN, SING!" a woman shouted on a sunny Thursday in May 1963 to black schoolchildren who were marching off hand in hand from the Birmingham, Alabama, Sixteenth Street Baptist Church.

And the children sang, "We shall overcome some day."

It was the first day of a peaceful children's march for civil rights in a troubled industrial city of 210,000 whites and 140,000 blacks.

At that point in 1963, the civil rights movement, led by Martin Luther King, Jr., was faltering. In Birmingham, the police had arrested hundreds of protesters. There were few left to protest. So civil rights leaders turned to schoolchildren.

"Birmingham in 1963 was about as segregated a city in the South as you can find," recalled a white Lutheran minister, the Reverend Joseph Ellwanger. "There were still signs over water fountains. There were no black clerks in downtown stores. There were no blacks in the police or fire departments. And there were a lot of open threats on the part of the police commissioner, Eugene "Bull" Connor, against any attempt to gain some of these rights."

The young marchers were in pursuit of their rights. Nine hundred children, from kindergarteners to high school students, fanned out in all directions in groups of ten to fifty. Some of them reached downtown Birmingham and marched right up to the front steps of city hall.

Connor's police chased the students down, piling them into paddy wagons, sheriffs' cars, and, eventually, school buses. The children sang and clapped their hands as the police arrested them. One little girl climbing into a paddy wagon was asked her age. She replied: "Six."

The charge brought against the children was parading without a permit.

Connor and the Birmingham Police Department were acting in the racist spirit of Alabama's governor, George C. Wallace, who had said at his inauguration the previous January: "I say segregation now . . . segregation tomorrow . . . segregation forever."

As Patricia Harris, one of the children who marched, said later: "I was afraid of getting hurt, but still I was willing to march on to have justice done."

On the second day, Friday, Connor was determined to keep the children penned in the black section of the city. With six hundred children in custody, there was no more room in jail. He waited on a nearby street with a dozen policemen and Birmingham's outgoing mayor, Arthur Hanes.

Squinting under his straw hat in the strong sun, the mayor watched for the young demonstrators to leave the Baptist church for another day of protest. At one o'clock, the mayor shouted, "Here they come!" and the police moved to confront the first wave of fifty children.

The police held them at bay and took away their placards. But the waves of protesters continued to pour forth, only to be met by fire engines and a warning: "Disperse or you'll get wet!"

One woman holding a four-year-old came forward to express the determination in the crowd, which was now joined by older teenagers and adults: "This baby is mine and he's in it too!"

Soon, the singing would stop and the screaming begin. The second-day protesters became defiant and angry. They confronted the police and the water hoses, which were then turned on. Special equipment harnessed water from two hoses into a single nozzle that sent out water with enough force to knock demonstrators to the ground and against buildings.

Bricks and bottles were thrown. More angry shouts. More bricks and bottles, this time from a nearby rooftop. A crowd of 1,000 to 1,500 adult onlookers was drawn into the turmoil when firemen in slickers and tin hats turned the hoses on them.

Then Connor turned his eight police dogs loose. The dogs lunged forward as their handlers pursued every black person in sight, including a fifteen-year-old who was watching what was happening. A policeman grabbed the boy and spun him around into the jaws of a German shepherd.

An Associated Press photographer who was standing nearby took the photo that told it all. The image appeared on the front pages of newspapers throughout the United States and shook the nation.

No words—and there were many condemning what happened— could match the impact of the photo described in the caption on the front page of *The New York Times*: "Police dog lunges at demonstrator during the protest against segregation in Birmingham."

When *Life* magazine devoted eleven pages to the Birmingham demonstrations, it began by stating: "The pictures on these 11 pages are frightening. They are frightening because of the brutal methods being used by white policemen in Birmingham, Alabama, against Negro demonstrators. They are frightening because the Negro strategy of 'nonviolent direct action' invites that very brutality—and welcomes it as a way to promote the Negroes' cause, which, under the law, is right. And they are especially frightening because the gulf between black and white is here visibly deepened."

The Associated Press photo sent around the world captured the depth of that gulf in the figure of the white police officer in dark glasses. His right arm grabs a young black man, his left hand grips the leash of a lunging dog. The long arm of the law is turned violent; a bloodthirsty dog attacks; a helpless young American is a victim.

A second dog waits, panting. A black woman seen over the policeman's left shoulder registers the terror felt on the streets of Birmingham. And in the upper left-hand corner of the photo, a sign urges, "Drink Coca-Cola," the drink by which America is known all over the world.

The dog—lunging diagonally across the photo—sent the message seen and felt by millions of Americans at the time, and by millions more around the world. It has been remarked that this single image and the outrage it provoked did more than the Emancipation Proclamation to promote civil rights.

A white lawyer, David Vann, who was in the middle of reform efforts in Birmingham, pointed out that the actual march for the most part never went more than one block. He described it as "a masterpiece of the use of media to explain a cause to the general public of the nation."

Referring to the "very dramatic pictures" created by the water hoses and the police dogs, he added: "The ball game was all over, once the hoses and the dogs were brought on."

What made the difference was the presence of cameras and a

horde of onlooking journalists from all over the world, including Japan and the Soviet Union.

The *Life* caption for its photographs typified reactions to the sight of racism: "With vicious guard dogs the police attacked the marchers—and thus rewarded them with an outrage that would win support all over the world for Birmingham's Negroes."

The episode's effects immediately rippled across the United States. In the following ten weeks, according to the Justice Department, more than 750 demonstrations erupted in 186 cities in both the North and South.

The country, the South included, was forced to look at the ugly face of racism, and President John F. Kennedy was forced to act. He went before the country and pressed for a civil rights act in words that paralleled what the justice-seeking student marcher said.

President Kennedy called upon the Congress to give American blacks not charity, but "the one plain, proud, priceless quality that unites us all as Americans: a sense of justice."

In 1964, Senator Jacob Javits presented an award to Charles Moore, the photographer who took the *Life* magazine photos of the water hoses and police dogs. His remarks summarized the history-making effects of the Birmingham photographs. He said that he knew of nothing that had had a greater effect in making Americans sensitive to the civil rights struggle than these "photographs which the American press and magazines have shown of actual events on the southern front."

"Because pictures backed up the words," the senator added, the nation faced up to racial injustice.

The children of Birmingham were seen, their cry for justice heard.

Viet Cong Executed (February 1, 1968) by Eddie Adams. Awarded 1968 Pulitzer Prize. Named best photo of year in the World Press Photo Competition. (*AP/Wide World Photos*)

· 4 ·

"The Picture That Shook the World"

■ ■ ■

Shocking the Home Front During the Vietnam War

IN SOUTH VIETNAM'S capital, Saigon, the Vietnamese were celebrating the Year of the Monkey in late January 1968. It was the feast of Tet, their holiest celebration.

In the United States, the public believed that massive American support was bringing victory in the Vietnam War. It looked as if the Viet Cong Communist guerrilla forces and North Vietnam were losing in their all-out attempt to take over anti-Communist South Vietnam. U.S. intelligence felt the same way.

As far back as 1961, President John F. Kennedy had authorized sending the first U.S. troops to support the South Vietnamese government. In January 1962, there were about 2,600 American troops in Vietnam. In January 1968, U.S. forces in Vietnam amounted to almost a half million men and women. A major part of all U.S. military power was at war in Vietnam: 40 percent of combat-ready U.S. divisions, half of the nation's tactical air power, and a third of its naval strength.

After more than six frustrating and increasingly bloody years, in 1968 it seemed that the United States and South Vietnam were winning the war. That's what President Lyndon Johnson was telling the country. General William S. Westmoreland, commander of the U.S. forces in Vietnam, added his assurance that the enemy "is certainly losing."

Then the Viet Cong surprised U.S. forces in Vietnam and shocked the American public. Viet Cong commandos attacked Saigon as part of a country-wide onslaught that became known as the Tet Offensive. Even though the Viet Cong suffered heavy losses and were repulsed, they showed that U.S. forces were *not* in control of South Vietnam. Even its capital was subject to attack.

The *Wall Street Journal* concluded that the "American public should be getting ready to accept . . . the prospect that the whole Vietnam effort may be doomed."

During the Tet Offensive, Viet Cong forces damaged much of the capital city, including General Westmoreland's headquarters and the presidential palace. They even stormed the U.S. embassy, where they killed five American soldiers before being turned back.

During the street-to-street fighting on February 1, Associated Press photographer Eddie Adams spotted Vietnamese marines escorting a prisoner. He was a suspected leader of a Viet Cong commando unit.

Photographer Adams followed as they pushed along the prisoner, whose hands were tied behind his back. They turned a corner, leaving behind the combat zone, and brought the prisoner to a waiting police jeep.

South Vietnam's national police chief, Brigadier General Nguyen Ngoc Loan, emerged from behind the jeep, packing a bone-handled revolver. He walked directly toward the prisoner.

"Loan gave no indication that he was going to shoot the prisoner until he did it," Adams recalled. "As his hand came up with the revolver, so did my camera, but I still didn't expect him to shoot. When he fired, I fired."

It was the reflex action of a dedicated news photographer. "Edward T. Adams lives and breathes photography," the Associated Press publication, *The AP World*, stated after Adams's photo won a Pulitzer Prize in 1969. "He is one of the most accomplished photographers alive, and he pursues opportunity relentlessly."

It was what Adams had done all his life, ever since he started taking pictures for his hometown newspaper in New Kensington, Pennsylvania. He was then a high school freshman.

Eventually, he became a staff photographer for his local newspaper, kicking off a career that included service in the Korean War as a marine combat photographer and twenty-four months in Vietnam for the AP.

At that moment on a street in Saigon, he photographed a shot heard around the world. Newspapers everywhere published the picture on page one. Associated Press general manager Wes Gallagher called it "the picture that shook the world." *Editor & Publisher*, the bible of the newspaper industry, said the picture caused Americans to take a second look at their country's involvement in Vietnam.

Historian John Morton Blum notes that the "brutal assassination . . . made an indelible impression of the brutality of the leaders of South Vietnam." He points out that pictures of the Vietnamese police chief as an "executioner" and of the Viet Cong enemy within the U.S. embassy compound in Saigon "made a permanent impact on the consciousness of many Americans."

The impact of the Tet Offensive, dramatized by television as well as photography, was immediate. Within weeks, public approval of President Johnson's conduct of the Vietnam War dropped from 40 percent to 26 percent. And approval for his over-all performance as president fell from 48 percent to 26 percent.

Amidst growing opposition to the war and his own growing unpopularity, President Johnson made a dramatic announcement on March 31, 1968. He was not going to run for president again.

When the highest-ranking South Vietnamese police officer raised his revolver, he aimed not only at a single enemy. He also aimed at the American sense of justice. Americans looked at the photograph and asked, "Is this what we're fighting for?"

Because photographer Adams was there with his camera, he transformed what would have been another shocking incident in the Vietnam War into an unforgettable image. Its effects were felt in the homes of the American public and in the White House.

The moment-of-death photo made Americans think twice about their attitude in going to war. They had always been con-vinced that they fought on the side of the "good guys."

It did not matter that Eddie Adams heard the general say, "They killed many Americans and many of our people." Viet Cong guerrillas had recently massacred a South Vietnamese colo-nel, his wife, and six children in their home. Years after the war, Adams heard from U.S. military officers that the victim was known to his captors as the Viet Cong lieutenant who had killed the colonel and his family.

What mattered was what the photo showed: a general killing a helpless man. The photo made a here-and-now statement: the general in uniform shooting a civilian in a plaid shirt . . . a man with his arms tied behind his back . . . the revolver at his head . . . the look of death . . . the dreadful retribution—on the spot, without a trial.

The photo's message is inescapable. The general's gaze and the movement of his arm force you to look at his victim. At the other end of the revolver, the expression on the victim's face screams with the pain of his final moment.

Not surprisingly, the photograph received six major journalistic awards, including the Pulitzer Prize and selection as the best photo of the year by the World Press Photo Competition.

The photograph's impact lingered. The antiwar movement in the United States seized upon it to promote opposition to U.S. military involvement in Vietnam. The photograph still can bring to mind the bitter controversy that the Vietnam War aroused among Americans. As photography historian Vicki Goldberg states, the photo "took on a meaning of its own."

That meaning is rooted in the shock of those who saw the photograph when it first appeared. It was a "terrible sight," as President Johnson's own speechwriter, Harry McPherson, recalled. He felt "the awfulness, the endlessness of the war" and "the unethical quality of a war in which a prisoner is shot at point-blank range."

Kent State—Girl Screaming over Dead Body by John Paul Filo. Awarded 1971 Pulitzer Prize (*Courtesy of John Paul Filo*)

· 5 ·

"A God-awful Scream"

· · ·

Firing at Students Protesting the
U.S. Invasion of Cambodia

ON MONDAY MORNING, May 4, 1970, Jeffery Miller was a twenty-year-old sophomore at Kent State University who wore his hair long, liked to play the drums, and worried about social injustice.

Mary Ann Vecchio was a fourteen-year-old runaway from Florida who was drifting through the campus in Kent, Ohio.

John Paul Filo was a twenty-one-year-old photography student working as a laboratory technician at Kent's school of journalism.

They were three individuals among young people all over the United States who were stunned by President Richard M. Nixon's announcement the previous Thursday. In one of the most provocative episodes in the Vietnam War, he had told the American public that American ground forces had invaded Vietnam's neighbor Cambodia.

The United States was still trying to end the Vietnam War. By May 1969, the war was killing thirty-nine Americans every day. At home, the country was bitterly divided between the "hawks," who supported the war, and the "doves," who opposed it. It was the most controversial war the United States had ever fought.

By 1970, the United States and anti-Communist South Vietnam had been trying for eight years to defeat the Viet Cong, Communist guerrilla forces supported by North Vietnam. As at other times during the Vietnam War, the American public had heard an optimistic prediction from their president as he announced American troop withdrawals: "We finally have in sight the just peace we are seeking." After hearing that victory was almost at hand, the public did not expect a widening of the war. But in private Nixon had said that a "bold move" was needed to support the Cambodian government in its fight against Communist guerrillas. So he invaded Cambodia with American forces, although he did not have the constitutional authority to do so. Only the U.S. Congress can declare war on another country.

In announcing the invasion, Nixon told the country that the United States was not going to act "like a pitiful, helpless giant." He added: "We will not be humbled. We will not be defeated." Nixon told the country that U.S. forces had invaded Cambodia in order to expel North Vietnamese who were aiding Communist guerrillas in that country. (As it turned out, when U.S. forces left Cambodia some weeks later, the North Vietnamese remained.)

While polls showed that the majority of Americans approved Nixon's leadership, millions of other Americans didn't. There were nationwide protests against the invasion of Cambodia on college campuses across the country. Kent State University was one of them.

At noon on Friday, the day after the president announced the invasion of Cambodia, Kent State students rallied to protest what Nixon had done. This protest was peaceful. At night, the students held a rally in downtown Kent. That rally got out of hand. A bonfire was lighted; traffic was blocked; and windows were smashed at fifteen businesses. It was a mob scene.

On Saturday night, the atmosphere on campus was ugly. A crowd of students set fire to the ROTC building and threw stones at fire fighters who rushed to put out the blaze. The governor of Ohio sent National Guard troops to the campus.

Sunday night produced more demonstrations. Two hundred protesters sat down at the campus gate and guardsmen had to use tear gas to chase them away. Meanwhile, on campus, guardsmen confronted more than a thousand protesters. With bayonets and tear gas, they broke up the crowds and averted trouble.

Monday began peacefully on campus. But as the *Akron Beacon Journal* reported: "After three nights of rioting, everybody on both sides of that deadly confrontation knew that anything could happen."

At noon, when the campus bell tolled, students assembled for another protest rally. They stood face to face with about seventy-five National Guardsmen. It was a weird sight: students in jeans facing guardsmen wearing helmets and gas masks. The guardsmen had bayonets on rifles that were loaded with live bullets. Two hundred yards separated the guardsmen and the students.

Jeffery Miller was among the students challenging the guardsmen, and John Filo was there with his camera to record the confrontation.

Suddenly, the guardsmen let loose a series of tear-gas barrages. Their bayonets fixed, they made a sweep across campus. Then they started moving to the top of a hill on campus. The crowd followed, shouting and throwing rocks at the guardsmen.

Filo, who was running along with his camera, described what happened next: "The Guard was moving backward, dodging rocks. As they reached the crest of the hill, they turned suddenly, dropped to one knee, and began firing directly into the crowd. People started running in all directions." At first, Filo couldn't believe the bullets were real. "I couldn't imagine live ammunition," he recalled.

The bullets wounded eleven students and killed four.

One of the four was a sophomore who was walking to class. One was watching the clash between students and soldiers. One was a freshman from Pittsburgh who the day before had placed a flower in the barrel of a guardsman's rifle and said to him, "Flowers are better than bullets." The fourth was Jeffery Miller.

After an officer ordered the shooting to stop, Filo turned around and saw Miller's body.

No one was going near the body, Filo recalled: "And then this girl, Mary Ann Vecchio, comes running up the street and she kneels down beside the body. I started walking toward her. Her body was shaking . . . she was crying. And then she screamed—a God-awful scream. My reflexes took over, and that was it. One frame."

The scream photographed in that "one frame" represented the anguish of antiwar protesters throughout the United States. Americans saw it on the front pages of their newspapers and on TV. The NBC nightly news program on May 5 forced Americans to look at the photograph on the TV screen. For seven seconds, the newscaster spoke with the photograph frozen on screen and then for another twelve seconds there was silence. There was only the photograph of a scream and a body on the ground.

In the photograph, students are scattered around as a backdrop. The body on the ground and one student standing nearby form an "L" that frames a single overpowering figure: Arms outstretched, shock on her face, a kneeling girl is screaming "a God-awful scream."

The single unforgettable photograph both captured and fueled the fury on campus. All over the country, hundreds of college campuses shut down as the result of student protests against the invasion of Cambodia. Antiwar protesters used the photo as an emblem. They carried large blowups of the photo with AVENGE written across it in giant letters that looked like they were dripping blood.

A special commission appointed by President Nixon warned that the Cambodian invasion had radicalized college students. Students regarded the president as dangerous. They were in a fighting mood. On the other hand, the polls showed that most of the country was still behind the president. The country was divided—and the Kent State photo showed how dangerous and disruptive that division was.

Robert H. Giles, who was executive editor of the *Akron Beacon Journal* at the time of the shooting, summarized the divided reactions: "There were those who felt that the student demonstrators had received exactly what they deserved and those who were quite ready to charge the National Guardsmen with murder."

There were also disturbing revelations. One guardsman told a reporter that he never fired at the protesters because he never felt in danger. Another reporter uncovered a confidential FBI report that said it was not necessary for the guardsmen to shoot.

For outraged students, the photo had one devastating message: Their own government had fired at them for exercising the right to protest.

For the victim, Jeffery Miller, shot in the neck, the Kent State shootings meant death before he could finish his second year of college.

For his mourner, Mary Ann Vecchio, it meant sudden and unwanted fame. Newspapers later wrote about how she was "haunted" by the notoriety.

For the photographer, John Filo, who won a Pulitzer Prize for the photograph, it was a moment when he was so "frightened" that, later, he was not certain that he actually had taken the photograph. "I was lucky," he recalled. "There were people killed on both sides of me. I don't know how I escaped without being hit. . . . It's something I'll always be thankful for."

Terror of War (June 8, 1972) by Huynh Cong "Nick" Ut. Awarded 1973 Pulitzer Prize. Named best photo of year in the World Press Photo Competition. *(AP/Wide World Photos)*

· 6 ·

"The Full Horror of the Vietnam War"

· · ·

Provoking Outrage Against
the Vietnam War

PHAN THI KIM PHUC was a nine-year-old girl living in a market town when a tragic mistake and a photograph made her a symbol of the horrors of the Vietnam War.

The mistake happened at Trang Bang, twenty-five miles west of the South Vietnamese capital of Saigon, on June 8, 1972. Communist Viet Cong guerrillas were holding the town and blockading Route 1, which connected the town and Saigon. For three days, the soldiers of the anti-Communist South Vietnamese government were trying to drive out the Viet Cong. But they couldn't budge them.

The South Vietnamese air force was sent in to attack from the air. The planes swept in low and headed for their target.

On the ground, South Vietnamese soldiers, women, and children were gathered along the road. They had taken refuge in a pagoda when the planes made a horrible mistake. They bombed their own soldiers and the women and children alongside them with flaming napalm bombs, which cover their victims with a gel that burns the skin.

Children burned by the fiery napalm jelly fled down the road scream-ing. Phan Thi Kim Phuc was among them, burned so severely that she tore off her flaming clothes and ran down the road frantically.

Huynh Cong "Nick" Ut of the Associated Press was doing what he always did as a combat photographer: He was traveling the countryside on foot to photograph the war up close. He saw the fire and the frenzy and he photographed what happened on Route 1.

His photograph was shown on network television and printed in daily newspapers throughout the United States. The horrors of the Vietnam War again landed in the homes of millions of Americans.

The effect of the photograph is devastating: burning children, run-ning from the horrors of war—South Vietnamese victims of a tragic mistake by South Vietnamese forces, which the United States supported and supplied.

The photograph rushes at you. First, the screaming boy is almost out of the photograph. Then the naked girl, her arms outstretched, her face filled with terror, fills the center. Two other children complete a diagonal line of horror that runs along the foreground of the photograph. Coming up behind are the men of war, in uniform, with helmets, carrying guns— a strong contrast with the helpless boys and girls who are victims of a mistake.

TV anchorman Walter Cronkite later stated that this photograph, and the one of the South Vietnamese police chief shooting a prisoner, "helped raise questions about the morality of a distant war."

When *Life* magazine looked back on all the photographs taken during the 1970s, it described the impact of seeing the burning children. "This 1972 photograph—more than any other single image—made America conscious of the full horror of the Vietnam War."

For the South Vietnamese photographer, the horror of the Vietnam War was personal. Only twenty-two when he took the photograph, Nick Ut had come of age during the war. His older brother, also an AP combat photographer, was killed while on assignment. Before taking the photograph, Nick Ut had been wounded three times as a combat photographer. As he said simply: "I'm a photographer in the field. Wherever the action is, I want to go."

Four months after taking the picture, he was wounded a fourth time, only a few feet from the same place on Route 1 outside Trang Bang. The next year, he won the Pulitzer Prize and five other major awards for the photograph, which appropriately was titled "Terror of War."

Ut later visited Phan Thi Kim Phuc in her village, where she had returned after fourteen months in the hospital and several operations. The Associated Press took a photograph of Nick bringing a box of children's books sent to her as a gift. In this photo, she is smiling.

As she grew into adulthood and struggled to make a life for herself in the years that followed, Kim Phuc continued to suffer from the effects of the napalm bombing. She was afflicted with fever and headaches, sudden panic, and an inability to concentrate. This prevented her from fulfilling her goal of becoming a doctor. Later on, in 1986, she moved to Cuba with the aim of becoming a pharmacologist.

Meanwhile, the war and its images continued to haunt the United States, though a cease-fire in January 1973 marked the end of the twenty-year armed struggle by the United States and South Vietnam against Communist forces.

Besides counting the cost of the war in billions of dollars, the United States military counted its dead and wounded. The final casualty figures showed: 47,072 deaths in hostile action; 10,435 deaths in nonhostile action; 153,329 wounded who needed hospitalization; 150,375 wounded who did not need hospitalization.

As Ut's photograph continues to evoke the emotions surrounding the Vietnam War, it does more than depict a tragedy that happened one day in June in a faraway war. It affects the way its viewers think and feel about war itself and the price war exacts in human suffering.

Earthrise (December 24, 1968) by astronaut
William A. Anders. (*Courtesy of NASA*)

· 7 ·

"Fragile Christmas-Tree Ball . . . Handle with . . . Care"

■   ■   ■

Showing Planet Earth as a "Little Spaceship"

EARLY IN THE morning of Christmas Eve 1968, three astronauts in the *Apollo 8* spacecraft were seventy-nine miles above the surface of the Moon.

In space, they were three solitary Americans.

On Earth, they were supported by the greatest task force ever mobilized for a peaceful purpose. A $33 billion space program had pulled together 20,000 contractors and 300,000 engineers, technicians, and workers to attempt to land a man on the moon. *Apollo 8* was a history-making step toward that goal.

The *Apollo 8* mission would check out spacecraft technology and the route that would be used for a lunar landing. It would also gather information about the moon, including information on possible landing sites.

While *Apollo 8* hovered above the moon, the mission faced its major decision:

Should the astronauts return to Earth, or should they enter into orbit around the moon?

If they reduced the speed of their spacecraft, they would come under the control of the moon's gravitational pull and begin lunar orbiting. Once in orbit, they would depend on their propulsion system to escape lunar gravity. If their propulsion system failed, they would be unable to leave the orbit and return to Earth. *Apollo 8*'s commander, Frank Borman, and his fellow astronauts, James A. Lovell, Jr., and William A. Anders, then would be stranded in space.

Before entering into orbit, all systems on the spacecraft had to check out perfectly. When they did, the decision was made to enter lunar orbit.

Around the world (according to *TV Guide*), nearly a billion persons in sixty-four countries waited to learn whether the *Apollo 8* spacecraft had gone into lunar orbit. Because the spacecraft went behind the moon, communication with earth went silent.

The world waited ten long minutes before contact resumed. In announcing that *Apollo 8* had gone into orbit, a spokesman for Mission Control of the National Aeronautics and Space Administration (NASA) said:

"It's an historic moment. For the first time men are literally out of this world, under the influence of another celestial body [the moon and its gravitational pull]."

Then something was witnessed for the first time in the history of humankind.

As the three astronauts and their spacecraft came out from behind the moon, they saw something no person had ever seen. Humankind has always looked skyward to see the sun rise. The astronauts, looking earthward from space, saw the *earth* rise gradually over the moon's surface.

From a distance of 240,000 miles, the astronauts became the first to see an "earthrise." On Earth, the sun was setting along the terminator, the line that divides day and night. The celebrated "earthrise" photograph taken by astronaut Anders shows the terminator as a line running through Africa, with light above and darkness below.

To Anders, Earth, the fifth-largest planet in the solar system, didn't look like "a massive giant." It looked like a "fragile Christmas-tree ball which we should handle with considerable care."

Lovell described the Earth as "a grand oasis in the big vastness of space."

On Earth, commentators struggled to find words to capture the significance of what the astronauts accomplished and the impact of what they saw, televised, and photographed.

Time magazine named the astronauts "Men of the Year" for 1968 and stated: "They traveled a quarter of a million miles to orbit the moon—and they discovered earth. One world, all alone in space."

The magazine described what they saw: "little earth entire, a remote, blue-brown sphere hovering like a migrant bird in the hostile night of space."

The poet Archibald MacLeish said that all human beings could now see themselves "as riders on the earth together, brothers on that bright loveliness in the eternal cold—brothers who know now they are truly brothers."

A global audience heard Mission Control conduct radioed conversations with the astronauts.

Then, after a total of ten two-hour orbits, the astronauts faced the most crucial moment of their mission. They were in orbit behind the moon and cut off from communications with NASA. It was time to fire the engine that would enable the spacecraft to leave its moon orbit and return to Earth.

At Mission Control, Peter Bond, who specialized in writing about the space program, reported: "Once again the tension mounted; a failure now would almost inevitably consign the crew to a lingering death from suffocation far from home. The craft disappeared behind the moon, leaving ground controllers with nothing to do but cross their fingers and pray."

The engine worked perfectly. It increased the speed of *Apollo 8* so that it could break away from lunar gravity.

As the astronauts once again saw Earth below, they announced: "Please be informed there is a Santa Claus."

Six days after leaving Earth, the three astronauts splashed down in the Pacific Ocean near Hawaii. They were back safely on Earth, which was acquiring a new image. As the NASA history of the Apollo program reported: "As early as *Apollo 8*, flights to another celestial body brought a new awareness of the spaceship Earth and the need to preserve it."

This is the strong message of the "earthrise" photo. It says something that statistics can't communicate. Nor can words do the job of showing Earth in its celestial context. The photo speaks for itself.

Earth is a solitary traveler in the vastness of space, a spaceship that orbits the sun at 67,000 miles per hour. In the course of a year, it covers half a trillion miles around the sun and about eight trillion miles through the galaxy. Scientists report that as space-ship Earth travels through space it wobbles a bit.

In showing Earth on its journey, the "earthrise" photograph creates a new, indelible image of what it means to inhabit the orbiting planet Earth. Spaceship Earth has become a familiar idea to Americans. All of us are traveling on it together and must take good care of it. We depend on all its parts just the way astronauts depend on their spaceship.

In 1965, the U.S. ambassador to the United Nations, Adlai Stevenson, had put into words what the "earthrise" photo showed later, in 1968: "We travel together passengers on a little spaceship, dependent on its valuable reserves of air and soil; all committed for our safety to its security and peace; preserved from annihilation only by the care, the work, and I will say the love we give our fragile craft."

Some one hundred years after William Henry Jackson photographed Old Faithful in the Yellowstone valley, photography sent the same message about the glory and importance of nature. Jackson's photographs helped save the wilderness for all Americans when the U.S. Congress authorized creation of Yellowstone National Park. By raising consciousness, by arousing concern for the environment, and by stimulating support for save-the-planet efforts, photographs of spaceship Earth can help to save the planet for all living beings.

Index